children's HISTORY of THE POTTERIES

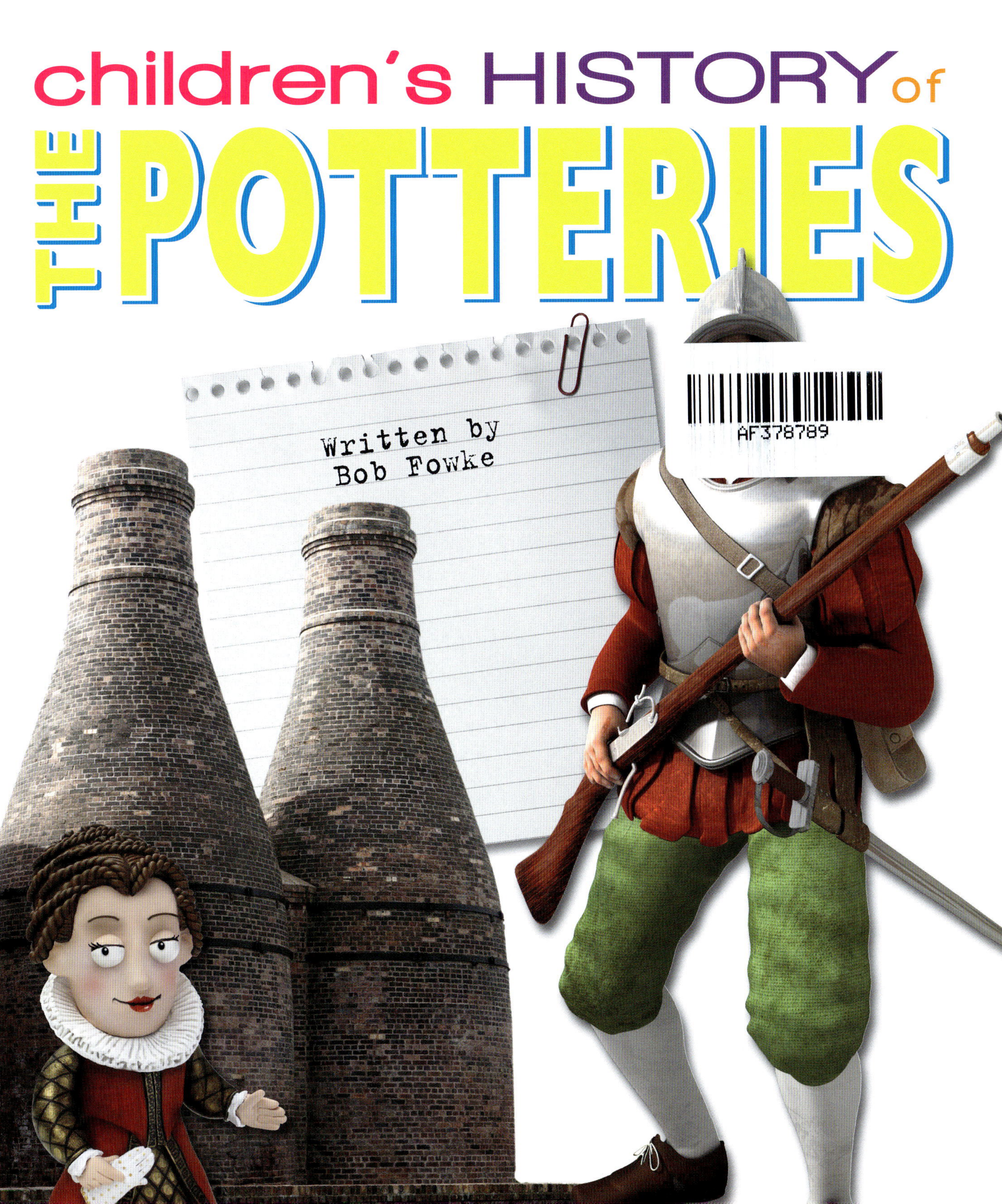

Written by
Bob Fowke

How well do you know your town?

Have you ever wondered what it would have been like living in the Potteries when the first bottle kilns were being built? What about working deep underground in the mines? This book will uncover the important and exciting things that happened where you live.

Want to hear the other good bits? You will love this book! Some rather brainy folk have worked on it to make sure it's fun and informative. So what are you waiting for? Peel back the pages and be amazed at what happened in your town.

Timeline shows which period (dates and people) each spread is talking about

THE FACTS

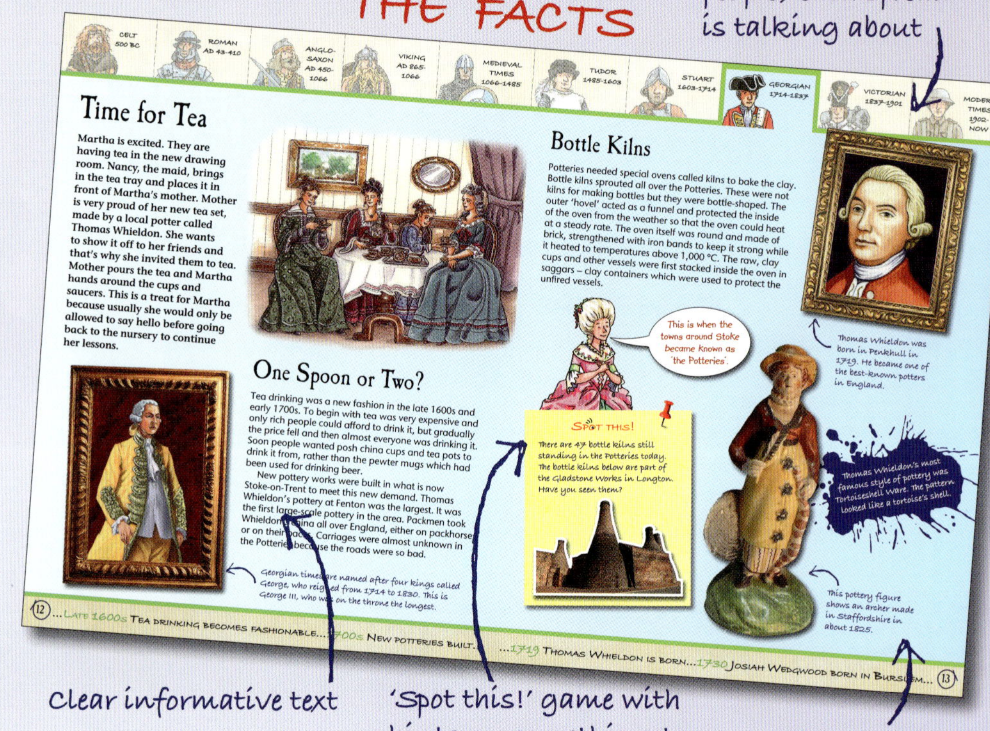

Clear informative text

'Spot this!' game with hints on something to find in your town

Hometown facts to amaze you!

THE EVIDENCE

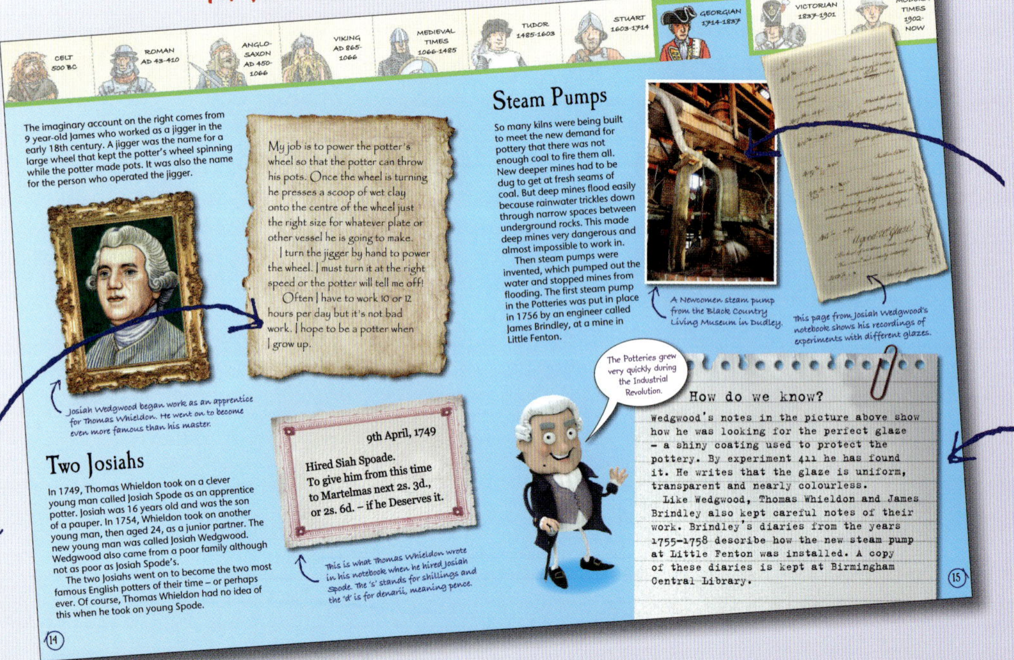

Intriguing old photos

Go back in time to read what it was like for children growing up in the Potteries.

Each period in the book ends with a summary explaining how we know about the past.

TUDOR
1485-1603
STUART
1603-1714
GEORGIAN
1714-1837
VICTORIAN
1837-1901
MODERN TIMES
1902-NOW

VIKING
MEDIEVAL TIMES
TUDOR
STUART
GEORGIAN
VICTORIAN
MODERN TIMES
AD 800
AD 900
1000
1100
1200
1300
1400
1500
1600
1700
1800
1900
2000

Contents

On the March

An icy wind howls across the long straight road. The soldiers bend into the wind. They are loaded down with weapons and baggage. This is wild country, where unfriendly Celtic tribesmen live on lonely scattered farms. A young shepherd watches nearby, ready to run and warn his family if the soldiers turn from the road. The soldiers are tired and can't wait to rest. They have marched at the 'common step' all day, covering 20 miles every 5 hours. Soon they will reach a small fort by the River Trent.

Boot Camp

Roman armies invaded Britain in AD 43. They conquered the Celtic Britons, including the Cornovii tribe, which covered the main part of Staffordshire. At night, if they were in hostile territory, each Roman army built a camp. They dug a ditch around the outside and reinforced it with pointed stakes. Many of these camps grew into towns.

Rycknield Street led from a fort at what later became the city of Derby to a fort at Chesterton, passing through the wild, half-empty lands of Stoke on the way. There was probably a small fort on the east bank of the River Trent near Trent Vale where soldiers could have rested for the night.

You can see Roman coins at the Potteries Museum. They show us the emperor who was ruling at the time, which helps historians to work out dates.

AD **43** ROMANS ARRIVE IN BRITAIN AND SOON CONQUER THE CELTS…

Lots of Pots

For 300 million years the area of the Potteries has been rich with a type of clay which is perfect for making pots. People have been working the clay for centuries. There were potteries in Roman times. The pots would have been distributed along the Roman roads, although the packmen who carried the pots had to make way for soldiers and government officials.

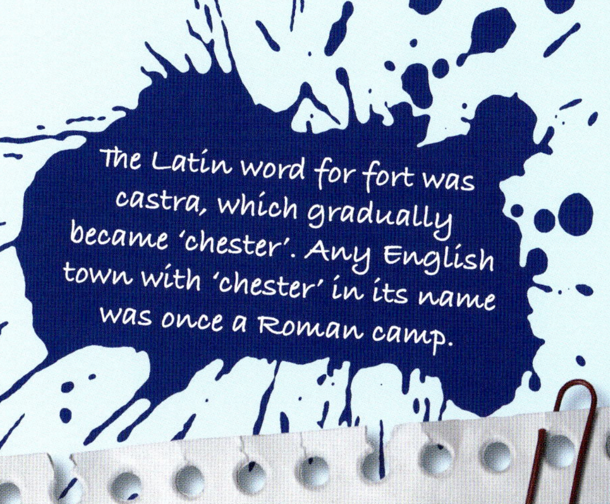

The Latin word for fort was castra, which gradually became 'chester'. Any English town with 'chester' in its name was once a Roman camp.

Things like pottery, coins and bones provide evidence so that archaeologists can work out where the Romans lived.

How do we know?

In the 1930s, some men were digging for clay in a deep marl pit in Trent Vale when they uncovered something very exciting...the remains of Roman pots and coins. This discovery led to a huge digging project in 1955, when the remains of a wooden building and a kiln were found, also from Roman times.

In 1970, workers building foundations for a new factory nearby, on the east bank of the Trent, discovered two ditches. Historians think these were probably part of a Roman fort.

A New Farm

Aethelinda is hot. Her dress is made from heavy wool. She is cutting bracken with her sister Hilda because bracken makes good warm bedding for farm animals. Aethelinda and her sister will carry the bracken back to the farm in a big wicker basket. Nearby, her father Edward and her elder brother are clearing woodland for a field. Edward is using an axe to chop the tree but sometimes he uses his seaxe or short sword. The seaxe is a good weapon and a useful tool as well. Her little brother wants a seaxe when he grows up but right now he has to help with the bracken.

Fighting Farmers

The Saxons were immigrants from northern Europe who moved into Britain in the years around AD 450–550. They arrived in the area that is now the Potteries after the Romans had left. The Saxons were fierce and warlike and there were many battles with the local Celtic Britons. Most of the men carried a short iron sword called a seaxe. Saxons brought their own gods with them from Europe but later they became Christians and, in the Potteries area, built a church by the River Trent. 'Stoke' was their word for 'place' or 'holy place' so 'Stoke upon Trent' means 'Holy Place by the Trent'.

SPOT THIS!

This Saxon preaching cross looks older and more worn than most of the gravestones around it. Can you spot it at Stoke Minster on Glebe Street?

Preaching Outdoors

When the early Saxons became Christian, some time in the 7th century, there were few churches for them to worship in. Instead, new Christian preachers worshipped on old pagan sites or at the remains of churches left by the Romans. Often, people gathered round a 'preaching cross' and listened to their preacher outdoors, in all weather. They soon built churches, at first made from wood but later from stone.

Stoke Minster's proper name is the church of St Peter ad Vincula. Inside the church you can find a font from Saxon times. It was removed from the church in the 19th century and used to hold flowers but now it is back inside the church.

The Saxon font inside St Peter ad Vincula Church was once used as a giant flowerpot!

The word 'Saxon' means 'a man who carries a seaxe' or, in other words, a swordsman.

Five out of six towns in the Potteries were settled by the Saxons.

How do we know?

Place names are useful evidence for historians. They tell us a lot about what places were like in earlier times and show us that all except one of the six towns of the Potteries were once Saxon settlements. Only Longton got its name after the Saxon period and means 'long enclosure'.

Town	Saxon meaning
Burslem	Burgheard's place on the Lyme
Fenton	Fenced place
Hanley	High clearing
Stoke	Holy place
Turnstall	Farm place

Fire Time

It is a bitterly cold night. Richard is a poor villein – a slave owned by the lord of the manor. He has very little land of his own but has to farm that as well as working on the lord's land for three days a week. His sons, Edward and Roger, are gathering coal from the surface to sell and for the fire. There is not much coal left on the surface. They will have to start digging deeper for it soon.

Sharing the Land

In medieval times most people who lived in the six villages of the Potteries were farmers. To make extra money, some made pots or dug coal to fire the pottery kilns. A few of them may have even worked full time making pots or mining.

Each village in the Potteries was surrounded by several huge shared fields and most families had the right to farm one or more strips of land within each field, growing the same crops side by side with other families. This was called 'strip farming'. They paid rent to the lord of the manor, either with crops or by working on his land without payment.

People in medieval times invented strange ways to 'cure' the plague.

How to Cure the Plague

Step 1: Find a live frog.

Step 2: Put the frog's belly on the plague sore or bubo.

Step 3: Wait for the frog to swell up and burst.

Step 4: Repeat with further frogs until they stop bursting.

...*1297* ARGUMENT OVER WHO DIGS COAL IN SHELTON...

Bell Pits and Adits

Coal has played an important part in the history of the Potteries. Where coal seams came to the surface, early miners were able to collect the coal without tunnelling. When the surface coal had all gone, they either dug short sloping tunnels called adits or they dug a vertical shaft with a chamber at the bottom. This kind of mine is called a 'bell pit' and was designed so that the sides wouldn't fall in. A winch and bucket were used to lower miners into the pit, and to get them back out again.

Look at this cross-section of a bell pit. Can you see how the pit got its name?

How do we know?

Shelton and Hanley once belonged to the Lord of the Manor of Newcastle-under-Lyme. Records of the Manor are kept in Stafford Record Office. Records for 1297 describe an argument over who had the right to dig for coal in an 'underground coalmine' at Shelton, the earliest record of coal mining there. There are also very early records of iron working at Shelton.

In 2001 a medieval hospital and 20 skeletons were unearthed during excavations before work started on a new lecture hall for Stoke City General Hospital. The medieval hospital had been there for hundreds of years, right up to the the 1500s. Some medieval pottery was unearthed as well. You can spot the pottery at the Potteries Museum but not the skeletons.

Country Life

The Bagnalls keep a pig at the back of their cottage. It eats all the scraps. Thomas used to take it to the woods to eat acorns but that's not allowed any more because the rich farmer won't let anyone use the land. The pig gets hungry. When the rest of the family are out looking for work, the pig pushes into the kitchen and Thomas is too small to stop it. Yesterday it ate all the broth. Mrs Bagnall was very cross and beat Thomas. By the looks of it, the pig will end up in the pot itself before long!

Henry VIII was the second Tudor king. Can you name all of his six wives?

Rich versus Poor

In Tudor times, rich farmers began to enclose the open or shared fields with hedges. They grabbed the land where poor families used to gather firewood and let their animals wander. Many families in Staffordshire were forced off the land and had to earn a living with small farming jobs and sometimes by mining or digging for clay. When there was no work they joined the crowds of unemployed people known as vagabonds who roamed the country.

A New Religion

Around 1530, King Henry VIII fell out with the Catholic pope over his divorce from Catherine of Aragon. He declared himself head of the Church of England and decided to close all the abbeys and monasteries. This is known as the Dissolution of the Monasteries.

In medieval and Tudor times, the monasteries took care of the sick and the poor. In Staffordshire, Dissolution meant the hospital had to close. If people became ill, there was nowhere to go to be treated. This was a tough time, especially for poorer people.

Crime and Punishment

Life wasn't bad for everyone during Tudor times but punishments for criminals were particularly harsh. One law of 1572 said that 'sturdy vagabonds' who refused to work were to be whipped and burned in the ear with a red-hot iron. If caught again they were to be hanged.

SPOT THIS!

In 1580, the local court moved to Penkhull to what is now the Greyhound Inn. Prisoners were locked in the cellars.

Civil War

In 1642, Civil war broke out in England. Several battles were fought between Royalists who supported King Charles I and Roundheads who supported Parliament.

Major General Thomas Harrison was a Parliamentarian born in Newcastle-under-Lyme. He was also the son of the town's mayor. Harrison fought in many major battles during the civil war and, in 1649, he signed the death warrant for King Charles I. When Charles's son later became king, Harrison was charged with treason. In 1660, he was hanged, drawn and quartered in London. Harrison is also known for only ever wearing red and gold!

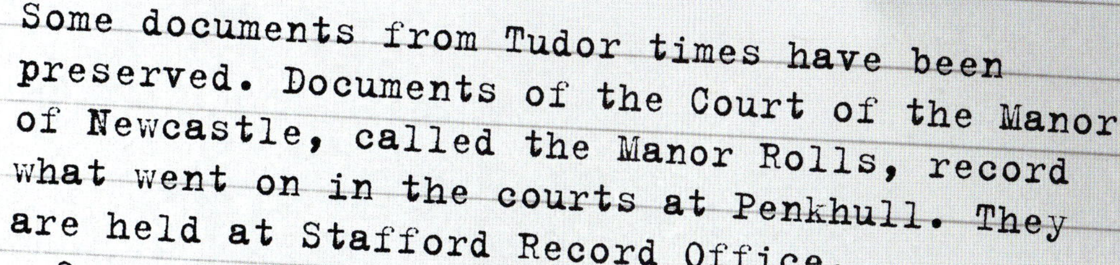

How do we know?

Some documents from Tudor times have been preserved. Documents of the Court of the Manor of Newcastle, called the Manor Rolls, record what went on in the courts at Penkhull. They are held at Stafford Record Office.

One story, from records in 1583, describes the trial for the attempted murder of a man called William Palin. According to the court's records, Mr Palin was attacked by two men with wooden clubs. He was ill from the attack for a month!

Time for Tea

Martha is excited. They are having tea in the new drawing room. Nancy, the maid, brings in the tea tray and places it in front of Martha's mother. Mother is very proud of her new tea set, made by a local potter called Thomas Whieldon. She wants to show it off to her friends and that's why she invited them to tea. Mother pours the tea and Martha hands around the cups and saucers. This is a treat for Martha because usually she would only be allowed to say hello before going back to the nursery to continue her lessons.

One Spoon or Two?

Tea drinking was a new fashion in the late 1600s and early 1700s. To begin with tea was very expensive and only rich people could afford to drink it, but gradually the price fell and then almost everyone was drinking it. Soon people wanted posh china cups and tea pots to drink it from, rather than the pewter mugs which had been used for drinking beer.

New pottery works were built in what is now Stoke-on-Trent to meet this new demand. Thomas Whieldon's pottery at Fenton was the largest. It was the first large-scale pottery in the area. Packmen took Whieldon's china all over England, either on packhorses or on their backs. Carriages were almost unknown in the Potteries because the roads were so bad.

Georgian times are named after four kings called George, who reigned from 1714 to 1830. This is George III, who was on the throne the longest.

Bottle Kilns

Potteries needed special ovens called kilns to bake the clay. Bottle kilns sprouted all over the Potteries. These were not kilns for making bottles but they were bottle-shaped. The outer 'hovel' acted as a funnel and protected the inside of the oven from the weather so that the oven could heat at a steady rate. The oven itself was round and made of brick, strengthened with iron bands to keep it strong while it heated to temperatures above 1,000 °C. The raw, clay cups and other vessels were first stacked inside the oven in saggars – clay containers which were used to protect the unfired vessels.

Thomas Whieldon was born in Penkhull in 1719. He became one of the best-known potters in England.

Thomas Whieldon's most famous style of pottery was Tortoiseshell Ware. The pattern looked like a tortoise's shell.

SPOT THIS!

There are 47 bottle kilns still standing in the Potteries today. The bottle kilns below are part of the Gladstone Works in Longton. Have you seen them?

This pottery figure shows an archer made in Staffordshire in about 1825.

The imaginary account on the right comes from 9 year-old James who worked as a jigger in the early 18th century. A jigger was the name for a large wheel that kept the potter's wheel spinning while the potter made pots. It was also the name for the person who operated the jigger.

Josiah Wedgwood began work as an apprentice for Thomas Whieldon. He went on to become even more famous than his master.

My job is to power the potter's wheel so that the potter can throw his pots. Once the wheel is turning he presses a scoop of wet clay onto the centre of the wheel just the right size for whatever plate or other vessel he is going to make.

I turn the jigger by hand to power the wheel. I must turn it at the right speed or the potter will tell me off!

Often I have to work 10 or 12 hours per day but it's not bad work. I hope to be a potter when I grow up.

Two Josiahs

In 1749, Thomas Whieldon took on a clever young man called Josiah Spode as an apprentice potter. Josiah was 16 years old and was the son of a pauper. In 1754, Whieldon took on another young man, then aged 24, as a junior partner. The new young man was called Josiah Wedgwood. Wedgwood also came from a poor family although not as poor as Josiah Spode's.

The two Josiahs went on to become the two most famous English potters of their time – or perhaps ever. Of course, Thomas Whieldon had no idea of this when he took on young Spode.

9th April, 1749

Hired Siah Spode.
To give him from this time
to Martelmas next 2s. 3d.,
or 2s. 6d. – if he Deserves it.

This is what Thomas Whieldon wrote in his notebook when he hired Josiah Spode. The 's' stands for shillings and the 'd' is for denarii, meaning pence.

Steam Pumps

So many kilns were being built to meet the new demand for pottery that there was not enough coal to fire them all. New deeper mines had to be dug to get at fresh seams of coal. But deep mines flood easily because rainwater trickles down through narrow spaces between underground rocks. This made deep mines very dangerous and almost impossible to work in.

Then steam pumps were invented, which pumped out the water and stopped mines from flooding. The first steam pump in the Potteries was put in place in 1756 by an engineer called James Brindley, at a mine in Little Fenton.

A Newcomen steam pump from the Black Country Living Museum in Dudley.

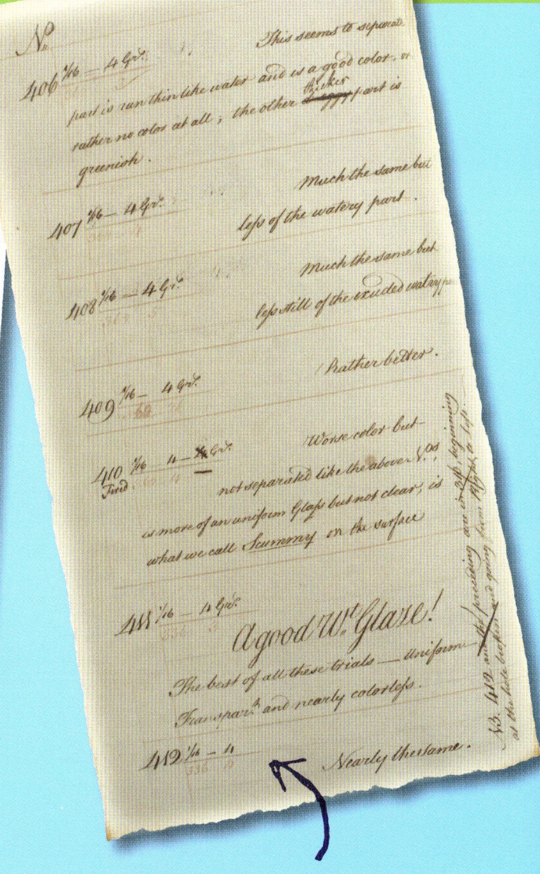
This page from Josiah Wedgwood's notebook shows his recordings of experiments with different glazes.

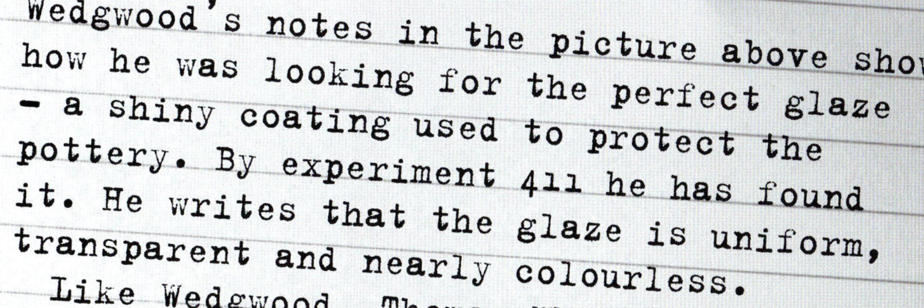

How do we know?

Wedgwood's notes in the picture above show how he was looking for the perfect glaze – a shiny coating used to protect the pottery. By experiment 411 he has found it. He writes that the glaze is uniform, transparent and nearly colourless.

Like Wedgwood, Thomas Whieldon and James Brindley also kept careful notes of their work. Brindley's diaries from the years 1755-1758 describe how the new steam pump at Little Fenton was installed. A copy of these diaries is kept at Birmingham Central Library.

Hedgehog Fritters

John is leading his horse along the new towpath of the Trent and Mersey canal near Stoke. They have just come out of a tunnel where the air was dark and damp. The new towpath is great but it doesn't carry on through the tunnel. Instead, the bargees have to lie on the barge on their backs and use their legs to 'walk' along the tunnel roof and push the barges through. It is a good life being a bargee. The whole family lives on the barge and at night they moor by the bank and cook supper over an open fire. Often they eat rabbit or hedgehog...delicious!

Canals

In a ceremony in 1766, Josiah Wedgwood cut the first turf for the Trent and Mersey canal, the first proper canal to be dug in Britain. James Brindley wheeled the turf away in a wheelbarrow. Other important people took a turn and then there was a big feast. The canal was fully open within eight years.

Josiah Wedgwood had supported the idea of a canal from the very beginning because the roads in the Potteries were terrible. Canals would be an excellent way to transport pottery. The journey was smooth and few pots were broken. The canal was planned and built by James Brindley working for Francis Egerton, the young Duke of Bridgewater.

Spot This!

This is the opening to the Harecastle Tunnel, designed by Brindley for the original Trent and Mersey Canal. Can you spot it?

Dots on a Map

By 1760, there were over 1,500 people working in the pottery industry in North Staffordshire. Large numbers also worked in the coal mines and iron works. The six separate towns of Tunstall, Burslem, Hanley, Stoke, Fenton and Longton were growing and starting to join up.

Etruria was Wedgwood's new pottery in 1769. Today it is the Etruria Industrial Museum.

This map shows the Potteries in 1775. The spellings of some place names were different then, such as Tunstal and Handley. Can you spot all six towns?

Etruscans

In 1769, Josiah Wedgwood opened a new pottery in Burslem next to the new canal. He named his pottery 'Etruria' and his workers were known as 'Etruscans'. For the grand opening of the pottery, Josiah put on a potter's apron and made six black 'Etruscan' vases.

There was a special village to house the Etruscans, with 76 houses. Most of the houses had two downstairs rooms with two bedrooms above. They had earth floors but were lovely compared to most workers' houses at that time.

Pottery was made at Etruria for 181 years. In 1940 a new factory was built in Barlaston, which they hoped would be better for workers' health. The pottery at Etruria finally closed in 1950.

These houses in Cavendish Street in Hanley were built for the Etruscans. But they wouldn't have had satellite dishes or wheelie bins!

The imaginary account on the right comes from a young lady who paints Wedgwood pottery in 1774. Each piece of pottery was painted by hand – a task that needed a lot of patience and care.

My name is Miss Parrs and I am employed by Mr Josiah Wedgwood as an artist. Along with my trusted colleagues Miss Glisson and Mrs Wilcox, I lead a team of skilled artists in one of the biggest art projects ever to be undertaken in this country.

In the past year we have painted over 1,200 beautiful views of British buildings including palaces and stately homes. Each view has been carefully painted onto a plate or some other vessel for a giant dinner service ordered by Empress Catherine of Russia. It looks wonderful, even if I do say so myself!

Secret Code

Wedgwood experimented with hundreds of different types of glazes and mixtures of clay in order to improve his products. He kept careful records of the results of these experiments. For several years, his chief helper was his wife, Sally. Josiah and Sally worked by candlelight in the evenings, sitting side-by-side on a bench.

Josiah wrote some of his notes in a secret code which Sally had to learn. Secrecy was vital because other potters wanted to copy their discoveries. Because of his experiments, Josiah Wedgwood invented many new types of pottery including Jasper Ware. Queen's Ware was another favourite. Queen's Ware was a shiny cream colour and was first produced in 1765 for Queen Charlotte, the wife of George III.

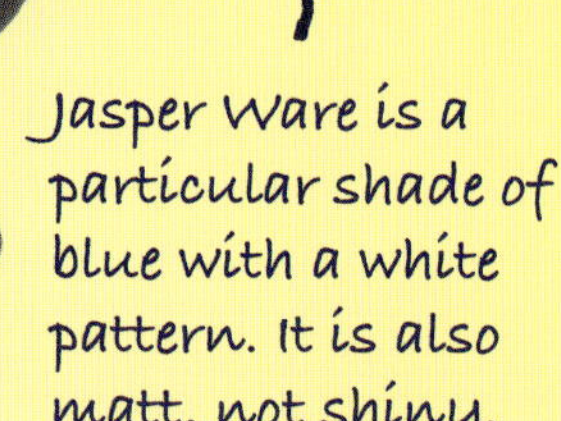
Jasper Ware is a particular shade of blue with a white pattern. It is also matt, not shiny.

Abolishing Slavery

Josiah Wedgwood was a member of the Society for the Abolition of Slavery. He manufactured hundreds of special china medallions which he gave to the society free of charge. These medallions were worn by fashionable ladies and other supporters of Abolition. A message inscribed on the medallion said: 'Am I not a man and a brother?'

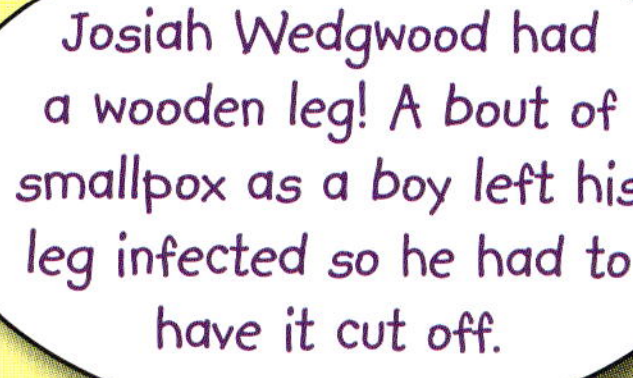
Etruria in about 1898

An Abolition medallion from the Wedgwood Museum

How do we know?

In 1906, 111 years after Wedgwood died, the Etruria Museum was opened at Etruria Works. Wedgwood kept a selection of his pots during his lifetime and this collection is held at the museum, along with lots of other Wedgwood pottery and six of Wedgwood's notebooks. You can see his secret code in the notebooks.

Many of the terraced houses built for Etruria workers are still there today. Do you know someone who lives in a terraced house? Do you know when your home was built?

Back-to-Back

It is the late 19th century and it's a dark morning in the Potteries. The air is filled with smoke from the nearby chimneys but people here are used to it. Coughing, they shuffle out of their little back-to-back houses and walk or cycle to work in the busy factories. Their shoes clatter on the cobbles and squelch through the mud and dirt on the streets. Mrs Appleby has just finished hanging out her washing in the dirty air. The clothes will not smell so clean by the time they have dried.

More Coal, Please!

Mine owners had to satisfy the ever-growing demand for coal from the potteries and from new steel and iron works. Coal seams near the earth's surface were all dug out so the miners needed to dig deeper. In the 19th century, the Potteries had some of the deepest mines in Britain.

Steam engines were used to power the winches that raised and lowered the cages which took the miners underground. It was incredibly tough work. Far below ground, hundreds of men, women and children worked in choking dust and heat, bent over in low tunnels leading to the coal face. There were a lot of accidents and many miners lost their lives.

...*1890* Josiah Wedgwood's home, Etruria Hall, becomes offices...

Steel

The Potteries were changing. Large businesses were taking over. The mines and iron works were employing more and more people. Shelton Bar steelworks now towered over the old Etruria Works. New railways took the goods away and there was no longer much need for the canal.

In 1890 Josiah Wedgwood's old house, Etruria Hall, became the offices for the Shelton Works and the buildings of Eturia Works sank low in the ground because the ground was weak from mining.

Etruria Hall was once Josiah Wedgwood's home. In 1890 it was turned into offices for the steelworks.

Arnold Bennett wrote several books about the Potteries, including Anna of the Five Towns. He was born in 1867 and grew up at 205 Waterloo Road, Burslem.

Edward Smith

Born in Hanley in 1850, Edward Smith was the son of a potter. He went to the Etruria Middle School.

In 1912, Smith captained one of the most famous ships of all time: *Titanic*. The ill-fated ship struck an iceberg on its very first voyage across the Atlantic and sank, causing the deaths of 1,517 people. Captain Smith went down with the ship.

A statue in memory of Smith was originally meant to stand in Stoke but in 1914, councillors decided it was bad luck. They gave the statue to Lichfield where it now stands. Lichfield has refused to give it back. Do you think it should?

Edward Smith spent 9 years working in a factory in Etruria before becoming a seaman.

Captain of the *Titanic*, Edward Smith came from Hanley.

In 1840, children working in the Potteries were interviewed by an inspector. The account on the right is a real story in the words of a 13 year-old boy called Charles Perry.

Below is an imaginary account from 10 year-old Benjamin, who works at the Gladstone Pottery. Can you imagine what it would be like to get up at 5 o'clock every day and go to work?

I have worked for Mr Clementson two years, and run moulds for William Trowton all the time. I sometimes wedge clay. Can't read or write, never been to Sunday school much; went to day school for a little while when I was younger, and left to go to work.

William Trowton pays me 4s. a week; we work regular six days in the week; master has always got work for us to do. I come sometimes at half past five, sometimes at six, and begin to light the fire. William Trowton gives me now and then 3d. more than my wages if I am a good boy; he sometimes scolds if I am a bad boy, he never yet flogged me.

I've got no father, got a mother, she's a painter by trade, but she's getting old. I've got one sister and four brothers, all working as potters; we all live at home, and keep mother amongst us. I go home to dinner and get sometimes bacon and potatoes.

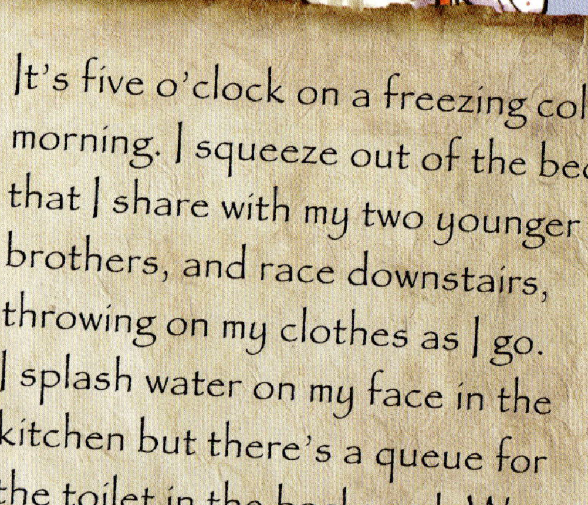

It's five o'clock on a freezing cold morning. I squeeze out of the bed that I share with my two younger brothers, and race downstairs, throwing on my clothes as I go. I splash water on my face in the kitchen but there's a queue for the toilet in the backyard. We share it with four other houses.

I give up waiting for the toilet, grab a slice of bread from the kitchen and run down the street. I work at the Gladstone Pottery in Longton, starting at half past five every day. I'll be punished if I'm late!

Chatterley Whitfield colliery was once the biggest coal mine in Stoke-on-Trent.

This is the Chatterley Whitfield mines rescue team in the 1930s.

The first camera was invented in Victorian times. This photograph shows Potteries author Arnold Bennett.

How do we know?

There are many relics of the mining industry in Stoke. The Chatterley Whitfield Mine at Turnstall was once a museum where you could visit the lamphouse, pithead baths and a winding shed. Sadly the museum closed in 1991.

We know about children like Charles Perry because of the written report from 1840. Parliament asked a government inspector called Mr S. Scriven to report on children working in the Potteries. Mr Scriven interviewed the children about their lives and recorded what they told him. Reports such as this helped to bring about Factory Acts in 1844 and 1850, which cut working hours for women and children.

Potters at War

It is a cold morning in October 1939. Men from the North Staffordshire regiment are catching the train to join the British Army in France. Their wives and families have come to the station to see them off. It is a very sad time. Little over twenty years ago, the scene was very similar, with the 'Potters' bravely leaving to fight in World War One. Just like then, nobody knows how long the men will be gone. And just like then, some of the men will never return.

Coming Together

The 20th century saw two world wars and some very difficult times. But before the start of World War One, people in the Potteries also witnessed a change in the way their towns were run.

In 1900, the six towns of the Potteries each had their own local government. It was hard to plan improvements and having so many local governments was a waste of money. So councillors began talks about joining together. In 1910, they finally agreed to join together in the new 'County Borough of Stoke-on-Trent'.

Cecil Wedgwood, great-great-grandson of Josiah Wedgwood, was a natural choice to be the first mayor of the new Stoke-on-Trent. But four years later, World War One changed this. At the outbreak of the war, Cecil Wedgwood formed the 8th Battalion of the North Staffordshire Regiment. He led his men into the Battle of the Somme in July 1916 but, on the third day of the battle, Cecil was struck by a bullet and died.

King George V visited Stoke in 1925 to announce its new official status as a city.

...*1914–18* WORLD WAR ONE...*1925* STOKE OFFICIALLY BECOMES A CITY...

Slowing Down

In 1925, Stoke was officially named a city. The six towns were still separated by green fields in many places, but they were joining up fast. Stoke was a big bustling place but it was no longer growing as it had done in the 19th century and earlier.

In 1926, working men and women all over the country, including the Potteries, put down their tools and stopped working, asking for better pay and conditions. This was known as the General Strike. Most of the Potteries came to a standstill. Some factories never recovered.

You can see a Spitfire plane like this one at the Potteries Museum.

Bombed Out

In 1939, World War Two broke out and German planes dropped bombs in air raids all over Britain. Stoke was a prime target for air raids because so many munitions factories and other important sites were based there. The main targets were the Radway Munitions Factory, the Michelin Factory and the railway goods yards. There was a lot of damage and many people died.

Reginald Mitchell designed the Spitfire fighter aircraft used in World War Two. Mitchell had attended Hanley High School. Today the Reginald Mitchell Primary School in Stoke is named after him.

Bizarre but Brilliant

Stoke struggled in the years after World War One but it wasn't all doom and gloom. Clarice Cliff was a brilliant designer who worked at the Newport Pottery in the 1920s and 1930s. Her pots became world famous and very valuable. She called her team of decorators the 'Bizarre Girls' after a style of pottery that she invented.

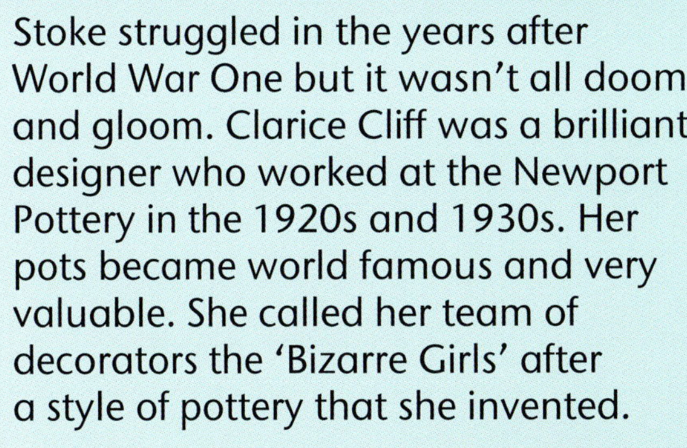

This imaginary account is told from the point of view of Peggy, a 12 year-old girl who lived in Stoke-on-Trent in 1941. This was a frightening time for Peggy's family and many other families around the country.

German bombers are coming. The wail of the air-raid siren wakes me up. Mum is at the bedroom door, holding a candle.

"Quick!" she says.

Mum drags me and my brother from our nice warm bed and the three of us run out to the Anderson shelter, in the yard right next to the toilet and the coal house. It is made of corrugated iron with soil shovelled on top for blast protection.

Mum tucks us up in the bottom of one of the bunk beds and clambers on the top bed. Our neighbours, the Johnsons, have the other bunk bed. Mr Johnson is very fat and he has bad lungs from working in the mines. His breath is wheezy. Mrs Johnson takes the other top bunk.

We lie in the darkness and wait. The bombers roar over.

"No bombs tonight, thank goodness," says Mum. "They must be on their way to Liverpool."

Everyone in Britain was given a gas mask in case the Germans dropped gas bombs.

Ration books contained coupons to buy things like food and clothes. Rationing carried on after the war, ending in 1954.

After the War

Even more damage came after World War Two. Employment in pottery factories shrank from over 54,000 in 1921 to 41,000 in 1945, when World War Two ended. The Potteries were battered by cheap foreign competition and, one after another, the mines also closed. In 1958, more than 24,000 people still worked in the mines but by 1998 all the mines had closed.

This cup and saucer were painted by Clarice Cliff's Bizarre Girls.

Some pottery is still made in Stoke today, such as the popular Emma Bridgewater designs.

How do we know?

There are many people alive today who can remember World War Two and the bombing raids. Perhaps your grandparents were alive then – or a great-grandparent? If they are happy to talk about it, you could ask them about their memories of that time.

Museums and art galleries do a great job of looking after proof of the past. You can see one of Reginald Mitchell's spitfire planes at the Potteries Museum, while other museums look after pieces of pottery by designers such as Clarice Cliff.

Photographs also provide evidence of the 20th century, showing what people wore and giving clues about what life was like.

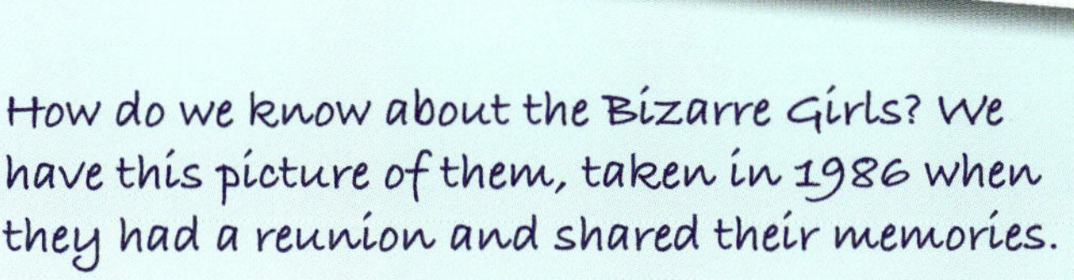

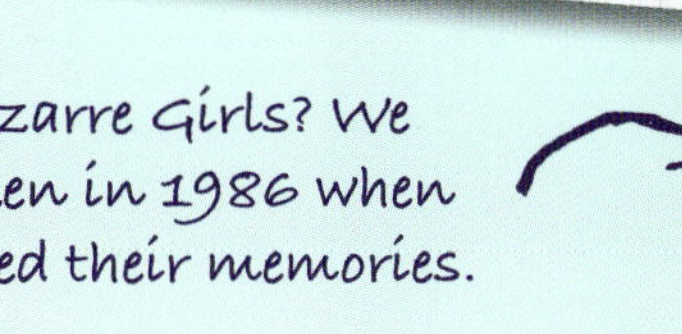
How do we know about the Bizarre Girls? We have this picture of them, taken in 1986 when they had a reunion and shared their memories.

The Potteries Today and Tomorrow...

The history of the Potteries can be discovered and enjoyed in lots of ways. You can see and touch objects at Stoke Museums, walk alongside the bottle kilns at Gladstone or speak to people who lived through World War Two. The important thing to remember is that history is really about the people who lived through difficult or exciting or dangerous times – people like Martha, Benjamin, Charles and Peggy.

Stanley Matthews is regarded as the greatest Stoke City player. In 1965 he was the first ever footballer to be knighted.

Stanley Matthews put lead in his shoes before a football match so that when he removed the lead, his legs felt lighter.

Stoke City Football Club was founded in 1863 and is the second oldest football club in Britain. In 2011, Stoke City won a place in the FA Cup Final at Wembley for the first time in the club's history. Although Stoke was defeated 1–0 by Manchester City, Stoke fans were passionate and gave their team an ovation after the match.

Have you seen this statue at Stoke City's Britannia Stadium?

...1986 1.4 MILLION TONNES OF EARTH IS SHIFTED TO BUILD FESTIVAL PARK...

Pithead wheels are arranged as a sculpture at Berryhill in memory of a mining accident in 1889.

Robbie Williams was born in Stoke-on-Trent in 1974. If you could be famous one day, what would you like to be famous for?

Part of the Garden Festival in 1986, this sculpture spent 25 years in storage before being unveiled again in 2009. Whose face is it? Turn to page 14 for a reminder!

How will they know?

The Potteries are bound to be very different by the time you grow old. How will people look back on us from the future? How will people know what the Potteries were like today? The Internet is a great way of recording what places are like. Photos, blogs and stories can all spread the word about our wonderful towns. Or maybe you'll be famous one day, like Robbie Williams!

Glossary

Abbey – a building where monks or nuns live and work.

AD – a short way of writing the Latin words Anno Domini, which mean 'in the year of our Lord', i.e. after the birth of Christ.

Anderson shelter – an air-raid shelter used during World War Two, made from corrugated iron sheets and buried in the garden with earth piled on top.

Bargee – a person who works on, or is in charge of, a barge.

Celts – a group of ancient peoples who covered large areas of Western Europe in the pre-Roman period and spoke Celtic languages.

Common step – a type of march for Roman troops which covered twenty miles in five hours. It was slower than the 'full step', which covered twenty-four miles in five hours.

Cremated – when a dead body has been burned into ashes, it has been cremated.

Fired – a description of pottery that has been baked in a kiln.

Font – a large vessel, usually made from stone, which is filled with water for Christian baptisms.

General Strike – a protest in May 1926 when around 1,500,000 people stopped work because of proposed lower wages and poor working conditions for coal miners.

Glaze – a glass-like material used to coat pots. A glaze gives colour and also helps to make pottery waterproof.

Industrial Revolution – a time of huge change during the 18th and early 19th centuries when inventions such as steam power and railways meant that goods could be produced on a much larger scale than ever before.

Jigger – the name for a device that turns a potter's wheel and also for the person who operates it. Today a jigger is also a type of metal stamp that shapes clay before it is turned.

Kiln – a special oven used to 'fire' pottery, baking the clay until it hardens.

Latin – a language spoken by the Ancient Romans.

Manor – an estate of land ruled by a lord, also the main house of such an estate.

Marl pit – a hole in the ground from which clay is dug for making into pots. Nowadays, marl also means a type of clay mixed with lime that is used as fertiliser as well as for pots.

Matt – not shiny.

Monastery – a place where monks live and worship.

Munitions – ammunition, weapons and military stores.

Parliamentarian – anyone who fought on the side of Parliament in the English Civil War. Also known as a Roundhead.

Pewter – a grey alloy (mixture) of tin, usually with lead.

Royalist – anyone who fought on the side of King Charles I in the English Civil War. Also known as a Cavalier.

Vagabond – someone without a fixed home, such as a tramp.

Villein – a type of slave who was bound to the land in medieval times and could not leave it without his lord's permission. Villeins had to work for their lords in return for the right to farm some land for themselves.

Index

CELT
500 BC
ROMAN
AD 43-410
ANGLO-SAXON
AD 450-1066
VIKING
AD 865-1066
MEDIEVAL TIMES
1066-1485